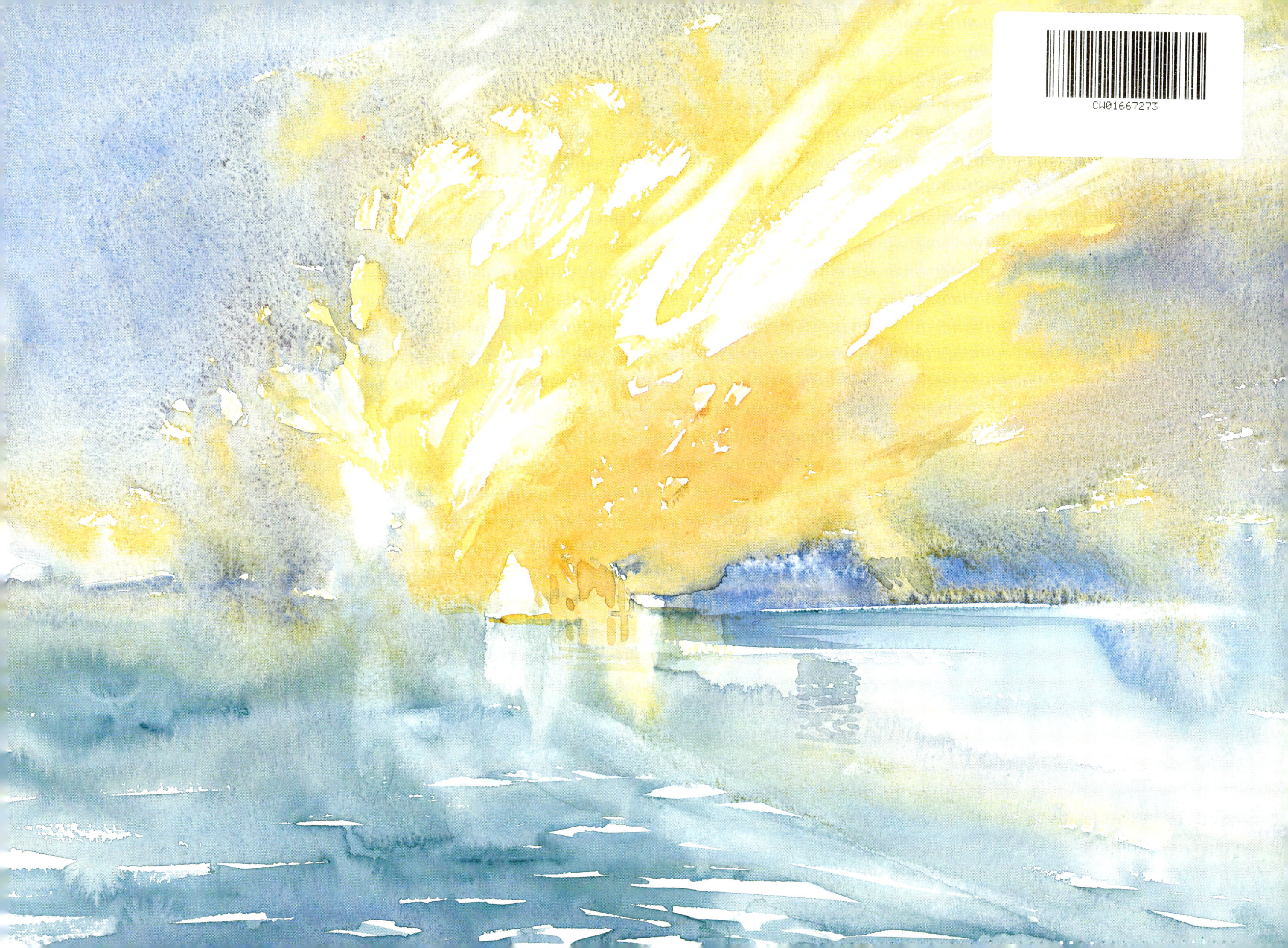

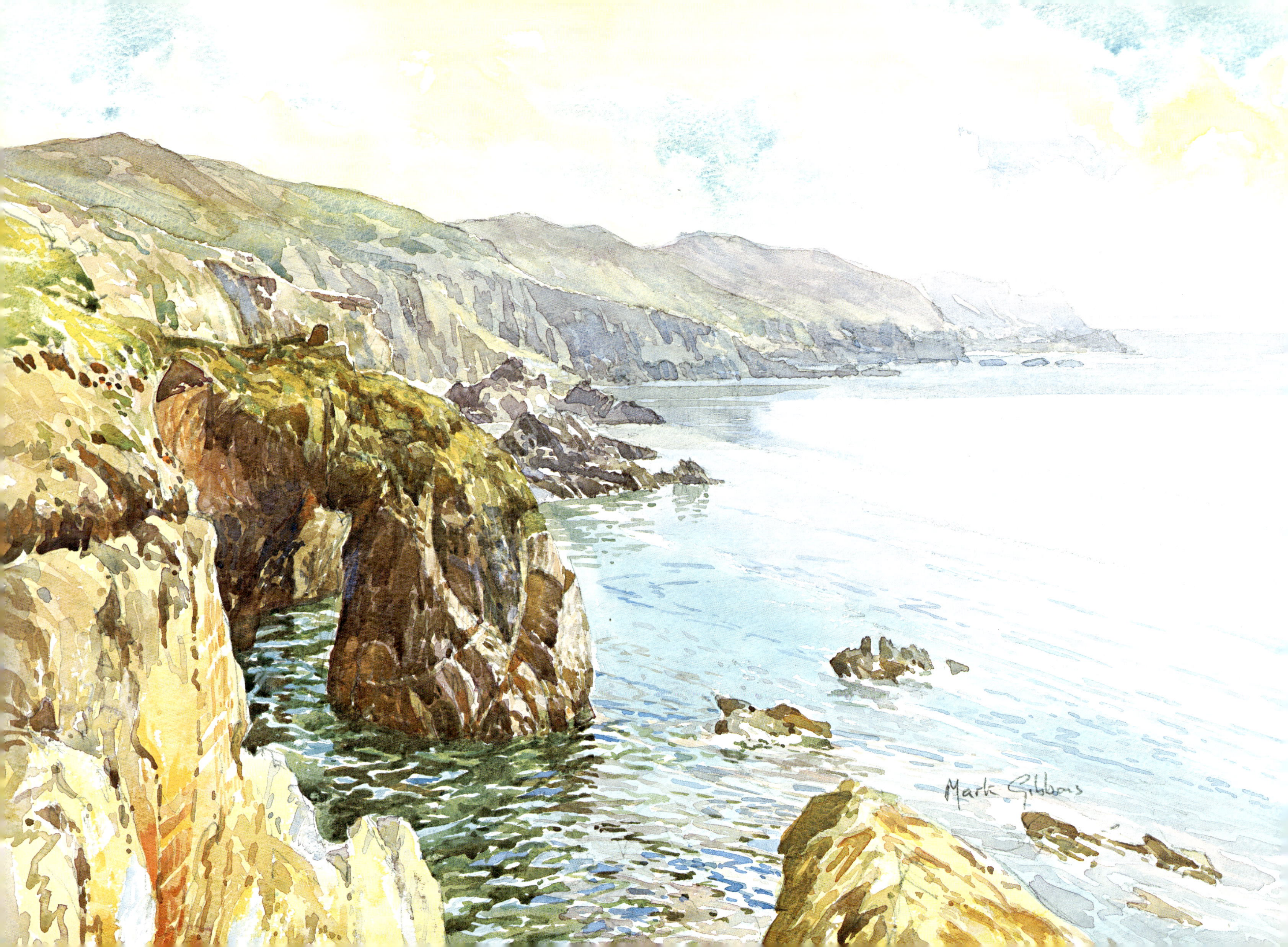
Mark Gibbons

The South Devon Coast

Mark Gibbons

Bossiney Books • Launceston

This book is dedicated to Alice and Sam, with love

First published 2001 by Bossiney Books, Langore, Launceston, Cornwall PL15 8LD

ISBN 1-899383-42-5

Printed in China

The picture opposite is a view from Gara Rock towards Gammon Head. The front cover shows low tide at Newton Creek.

Beer

Much of the character of the Devon landscape is shaped by the red sandstone in the underlying ground. The ploughed fields reveal it, cob walls and church towers are made from it, and headlands and cliffs – from Brixham east to Sidmouth and beyond – display its rich colour. Not until you reach Branscombe and Beer does the startlingly different white chalk appear. It's as if the land itself senses the county boundary a few kilometres on.

Beer is as far east as I went for this collection of paintings. It is a delightful little village set in a steep valley. A tiny stream runs along the main street that leads down to a natural cove, protected from the harsh south-westerly seas by the massive cliff running due south to Beer Head.

Unlike many of the small villages along the coast, Beer has managed to retain at least some of its fishing industry. The boats, such as the one in the foreground, are winched or towed up the shingle beach, with logs set beneath their keels to ease their way.

In researching this book, I found numerous stories of smuggling, with hidden passageways and caves in the cliffs around the cove. I would guess that if only half the stories are true, the good fishermen of Beer probably made as much money from contraband as they ever did from their nets and pots.

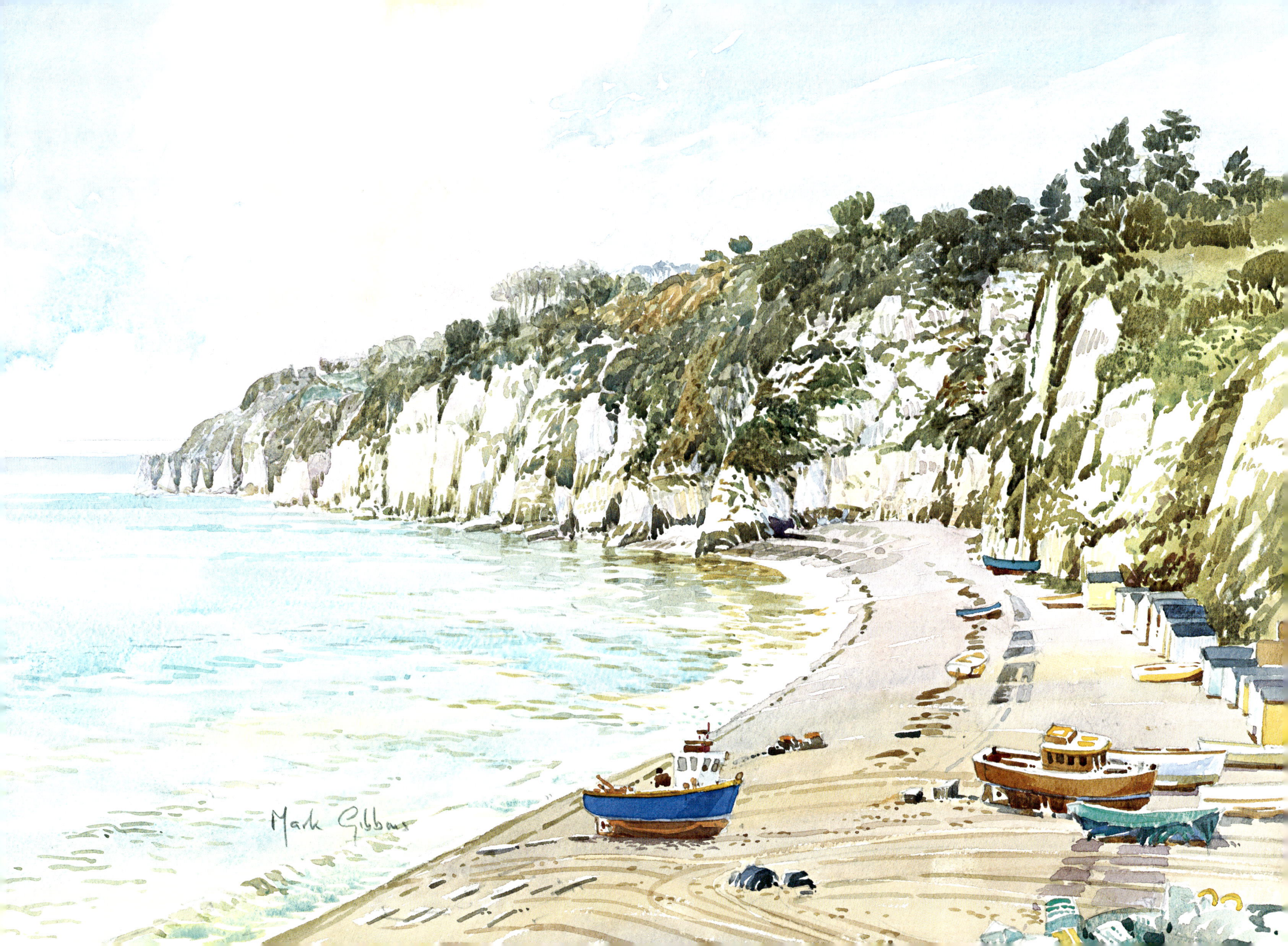
Mark Gibbons

Cottages at Sidmouth

From the late 1790s, the then small fishing village of Sidmouth began attracting distinguished 'incomers' who were searching for a kind of bucolic idyll. The homes they built reflect their idea of rural life and the wealth they brought with them. The cottages at the west end of the Esplanade, which I have painted in some detail, show some fine examples of their 'cottage orné' style of architecture: there are Gothicised windows, carved eaves and barge-boards, balconies and verandahs.

At the time these houses were constructed, there already existed several smaller cottages below them on the beach. They are seen quite clearly in contemporary prints. However, the great storm of 1824 washed them completely away – an example of the risks of building so close to the sea.

Though the wheeled landing stage in the foreground of the picture looks Victorian, it is still used during the summer season when boats take visitors on sight-seeing trips along the coast. In the background to the right, the tall cliffs of Peak Hill are plainly visible. It is a steep climb, but the view from the top is spectacular.

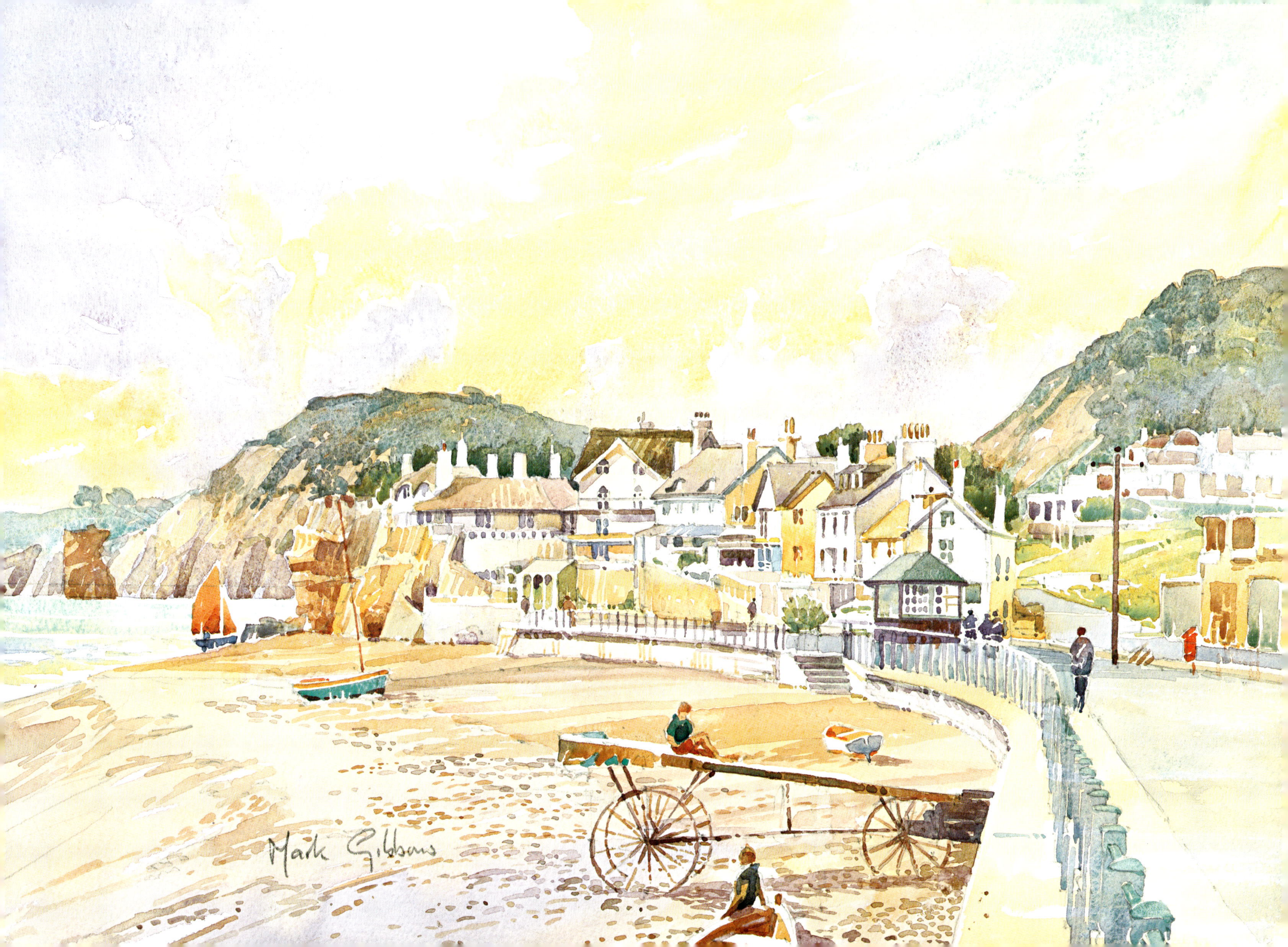
Mark Gibbons

West Down Cliffs at Budleigh Salterton

The South Devon Coast Path climbs steeply up from the western end of Budleigh Parade and comes out at the edge of the golf course on West Down. The picture shows the view looking back down to Budleigh, with the sweep of the beach curving round to Otter Head where the river Otter meets the sea. Far in the distance you can just make out the white cliffs of Branscombe and Beer Head beyond Sidmouth.

What I love about the landscape and what inspired this painting was the sheer expanse and rich warm colour of the local red sandstone cliff face. I don't know just how quickly the shoreline is moving north, but judging by the undercut vegetation and the fir trees about to topple over the edge it would seem that the erosion is pretty severe.

Budleigh has always been known as an unassuming, almost genteel, place. This can partly be explained by the fact that it has a shingle beach, while the sand at Exmouth just down the coast attracts hundreds of young families with their buckets and spades. I imagine Budleigh will remain as quiet as it is until children stop making sand castles.

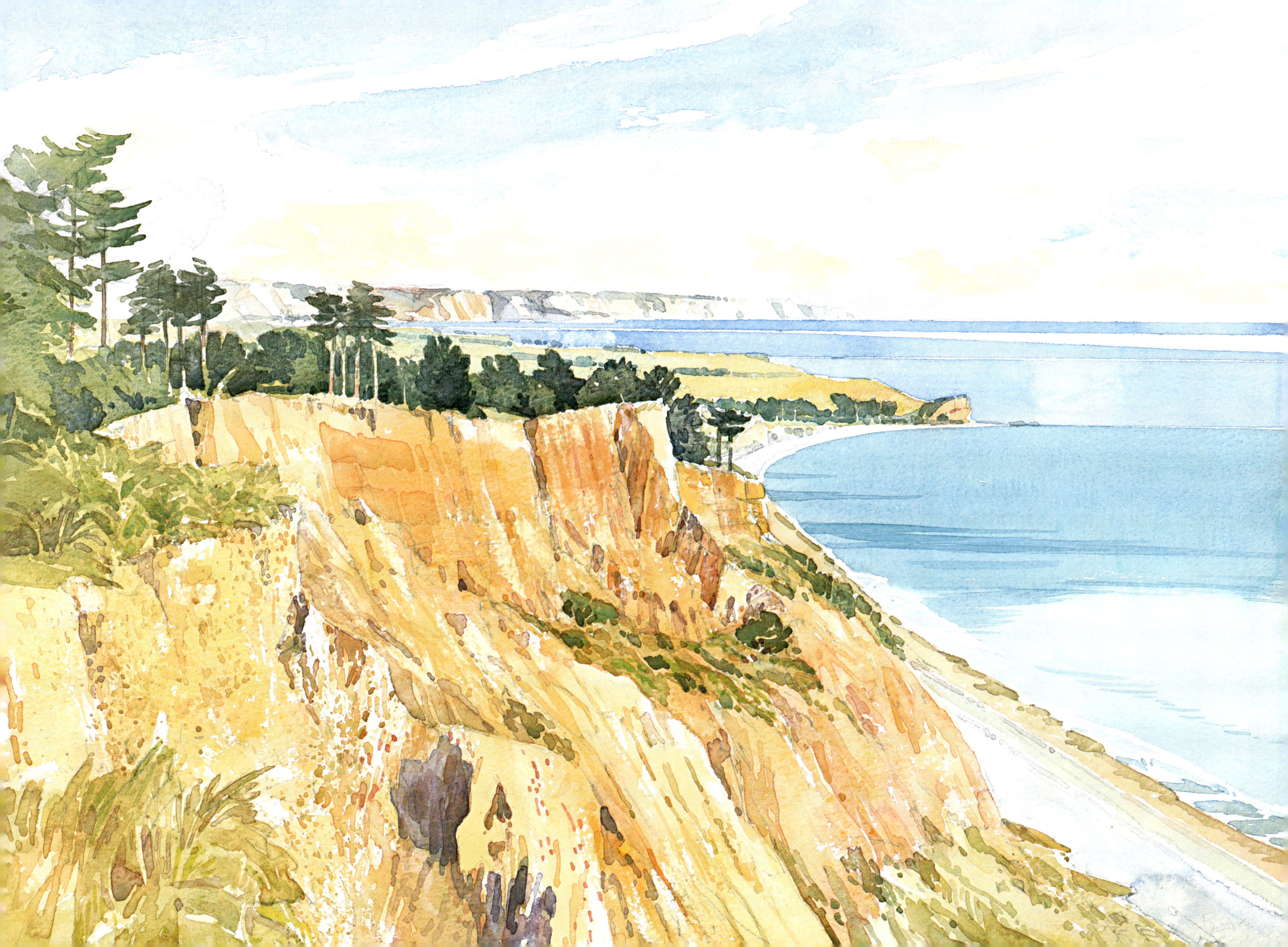

Sailing off Exmouth

Exmouth is one of Devon's oldest watering places. In 1750 a visitor said it was 'a place to which the people of Exeter much resort for diversion and bathing in the sea' – long before Torquay became popular.

The terrace of houses that can be seen below the tower of Holy Trinity Church is called the Beacon. It was built in the early 1790s for the fashionable and wealthy who were then beginning to visit the town – Lady Nelson lived in number 6 and Lady Byron in number 19. The promenade, begun in 1841 and extended thirty years later, is three kilometres long and stretches from the dock area along to Orcombe Point.

More recently Exmouth has been a favourite resort for families with children. A good deal of its appeal lies in its sandy beach, unlike the towns to the east which have shingle beaches.

The scene shows the view from the end of Dawlish Warren on a breezy summer's day. The warm brown sails of the old sailing boat contrast well with the cool Antwerp Blue of the sea and the Cerulean Blue of the sky – a colour scheme much used by the Impressionists.

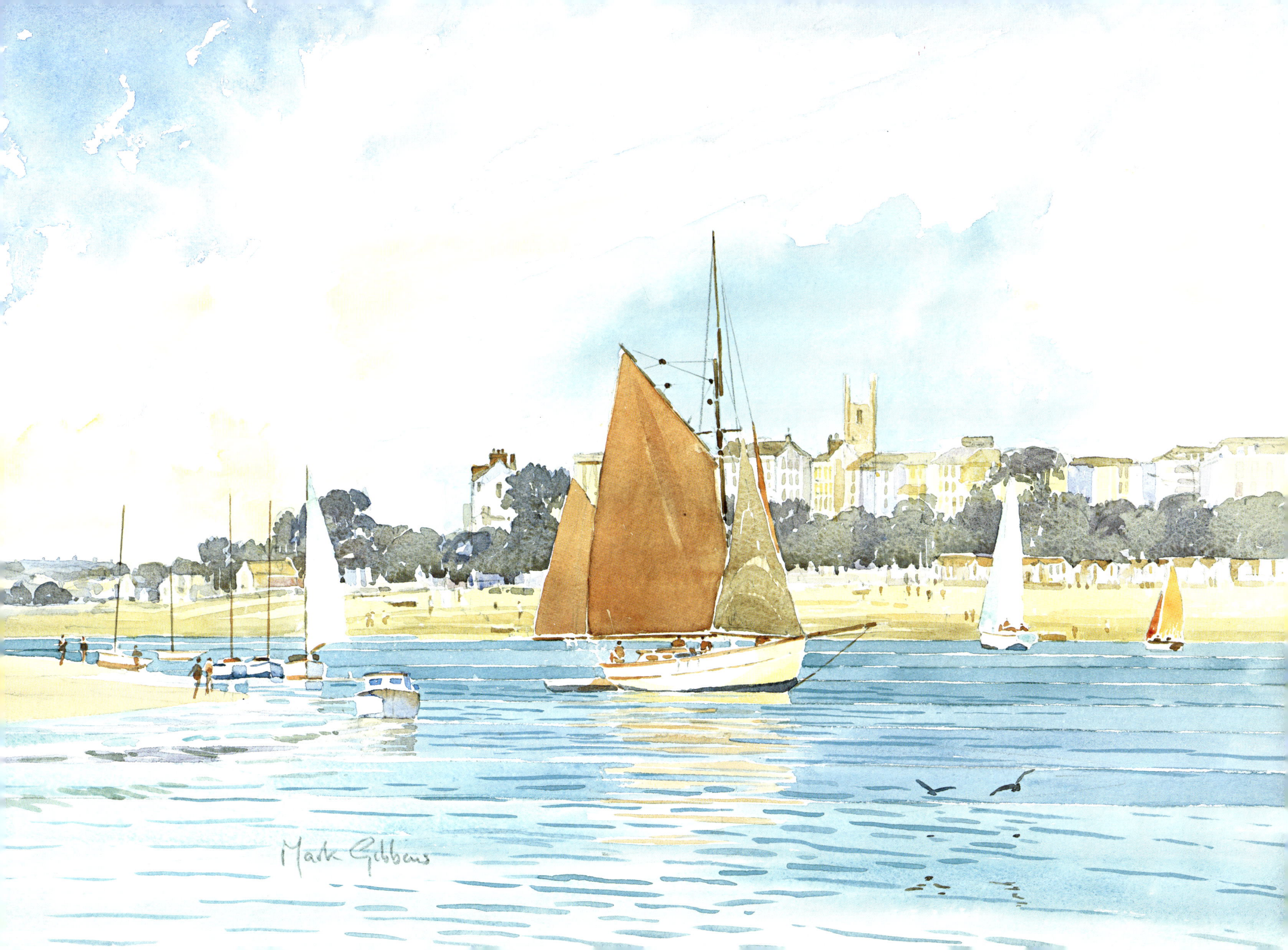
Mark Gibbons

Shelly Beach, Exmouth

The picture shows Shelly Beach at low tide. Although some would say this area is a little shabby, facing the mud rather than the open sea, I like it and always have done. It's near to the working end of Exmouth, close to the docks. Until recently it had a small 'village' of beach shacks with wooden verandahs that faced the late sun over the estuary. Perhaps the ground they rested on became too valuable, and sadly they have been replaced by some very expensive apartments.

There are still a few sheds left standing and I'm glad to paint a record of them, with their peeling paint and weathered board reflecting the last of the sun. I hope they remain for a few years yet, for they add vigour and charm to a spot which the developers seem only too ready to bury. Let me put it this way: I can't see many artists queuing up to paint the apartment blocks!

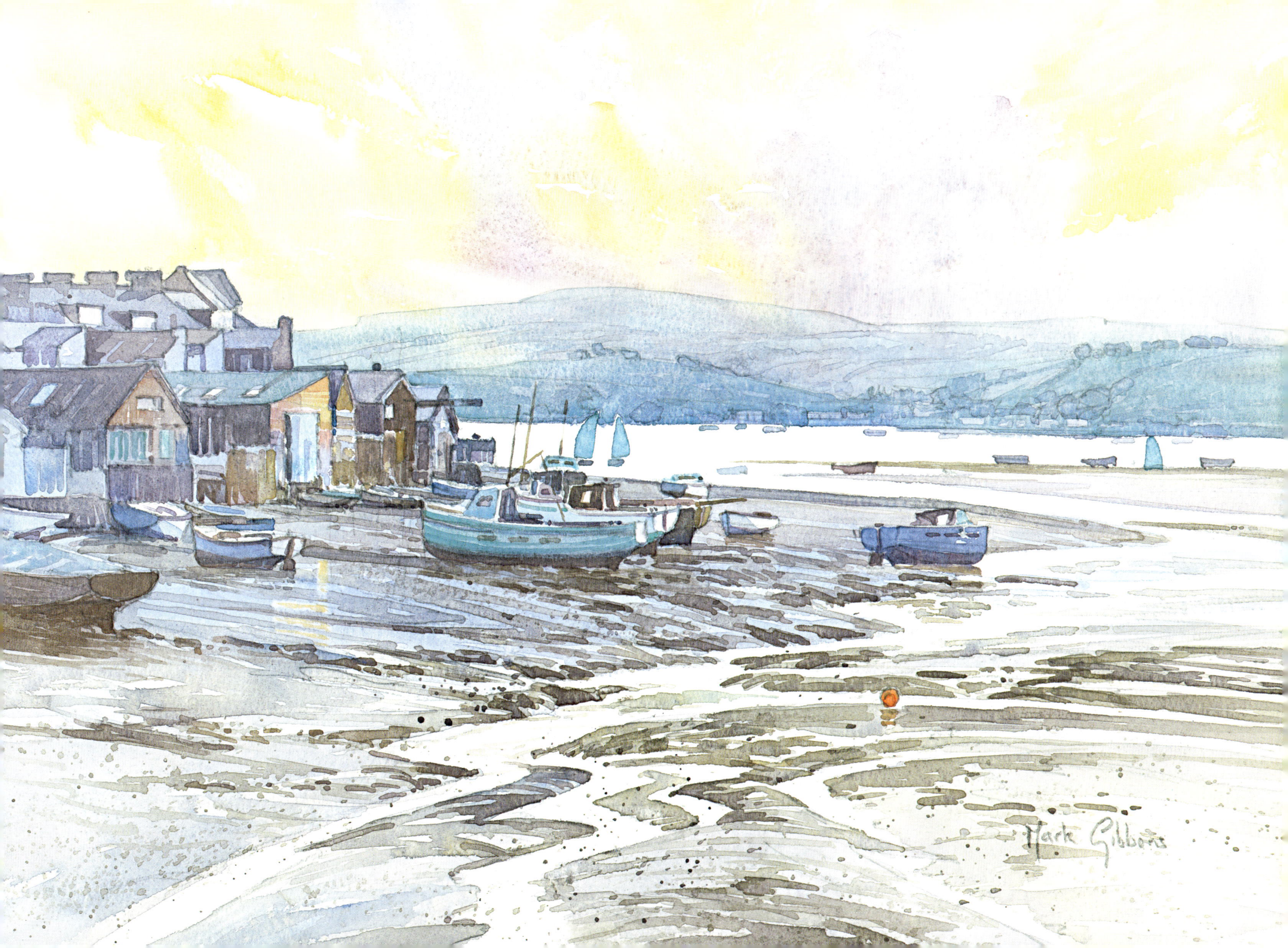
Mark Gibbons

Lympstone

I recall visiting Lympstone for the first time almost twenty-five years ago and being surprised to find a red brick tower on the beach which looked as though it would have been more at home in a small-scale Venice.

The tower was built by Mr W H Peters of nearby Harefield House as a tribute to his beloved wife Mary Jane and to 'commemorate her kindness and sympathy to the poor of Lympstone'. It was also a practical gesture, as the tower has a large clock high on its seaward side to help the fishermen work out the coming and going of the tides. (My guess is that the poor fishermen of Lympstone had been managing quite well for decades without the assistance of a clock.)

On that first visit the small harbour still held several well-maintained clinker-built fishing boats and along the foreshore a few nets hung between tall poles to dry in the salty air. Today the view from the shore across the Exe estuary is still a superb sight with the afternoon sun sparkling on the water and Powderham Castle silhouetted on the skyline.

The harbour is now home to a thriving sailing club and during the summer, when the tide is right in, dozens of dinghies take to the water. The poles haven't disappeared, but the nets have gone and in their place bright washing flutters in the sea breeze.

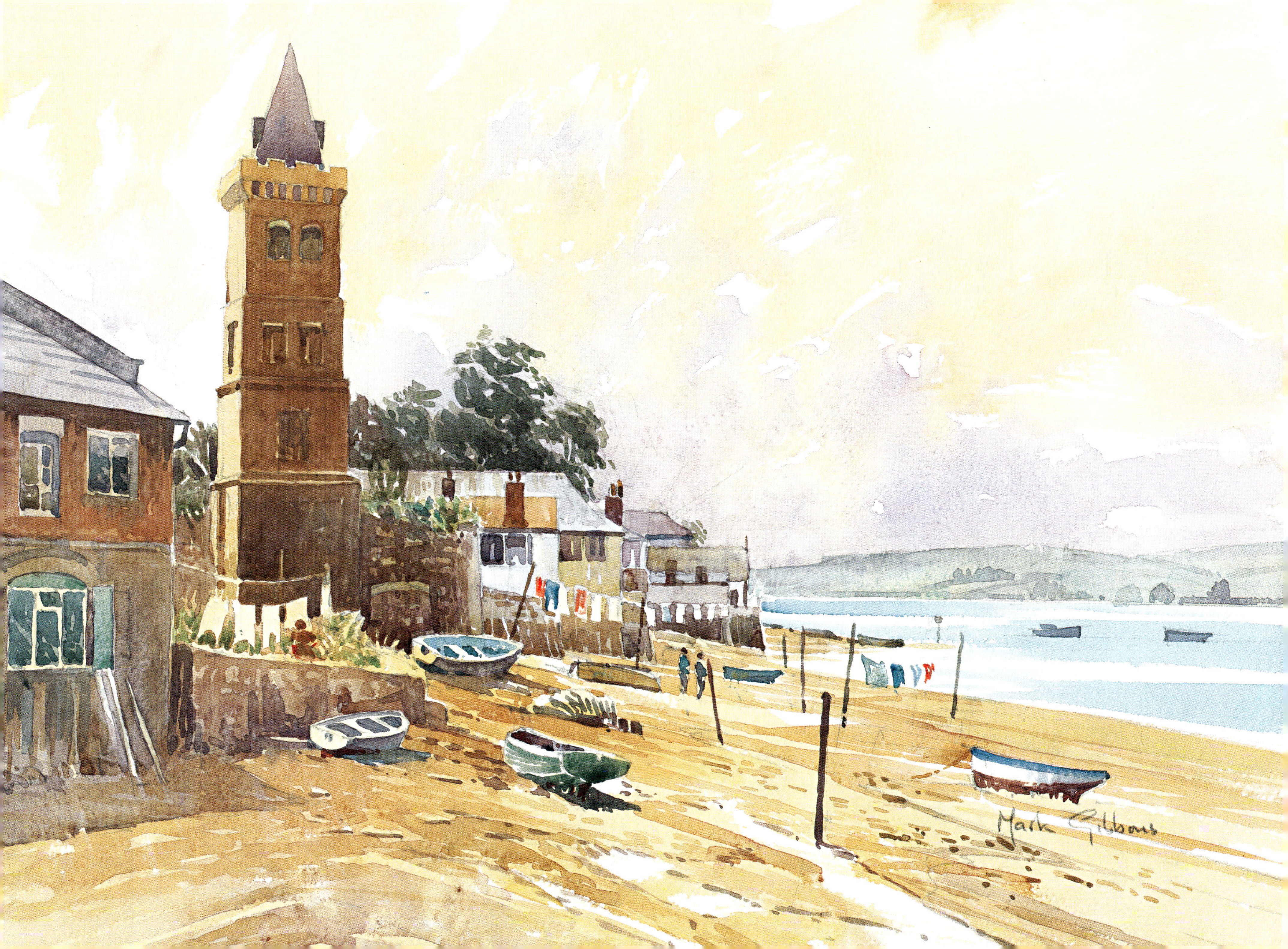
Mark Gibbons

Evening light, Topsham

Built on high ground to the back of the quay, Topsham Church, with its red sandstone tower, acts as a distinct landmark in the upper reaches of the Exe estuary. From the churchyard you can find some of the most beautiful and extensive views of the water. I have painted the scene in evening light, looking north-west towards the distant hills over the tiled rooftop of 'Wixells', one of Topsham's loveliest river-side houses.

Ever since Roman times Topsham has been a thriving port, and in the early 1700s there was a strong trading link with Holland. Topsham exported Devon's well-made woollen cloth and other goods, and many of the Dutch merchants settled in the town. They left their mark in the form of round gables and hanging slates on the houses they erected. Interestingly, a number of these buildings were constructed from the bricks that were used as ballast on the ships crossing from Holland, and can be seen today in the Strand and Ferry Road.

On the far side of the estuary you can see Topsham Lock with its lock-keeper's cottage. The ship canal, which can be glimpsed just behind the dwelling, was built in 1567 and runs from Exeter to Turf Lock, about half-way down the estuary. It went out of commission in 1960, but is still used occasionally by small pleasure craft.

To my eyes, this scene is one of the most attractive on the Exe, and is especially poignant because it holds so many echoes of Topsham's long and rich maritime past.

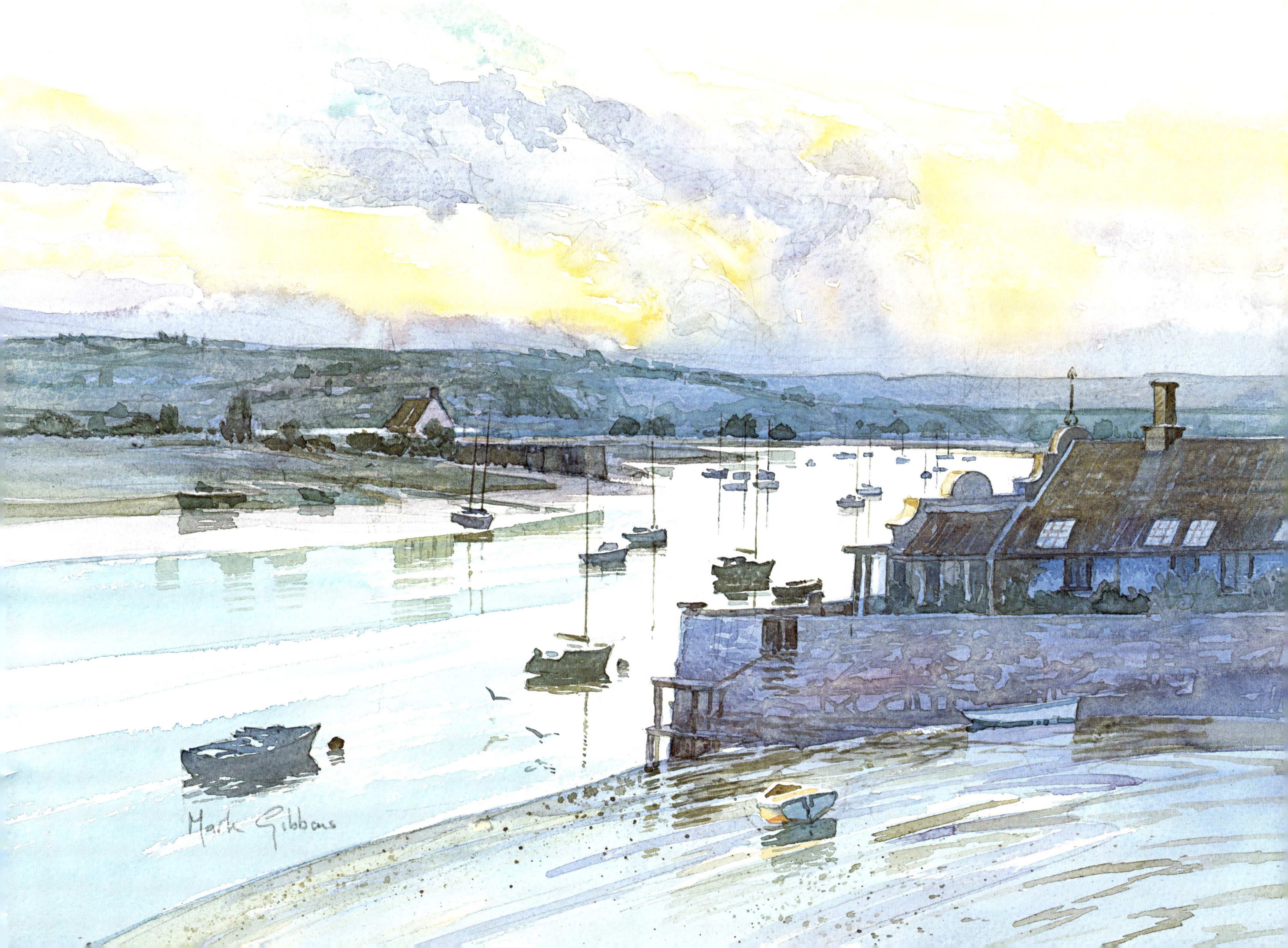
Mark Gibbons

The Teign Estuary

Sometimes I go out looking for places to paint, hunting them as though they were an elusive quarry, but every now and then it is the view which pounces on me.

One summer's evening I was driving on the road between Newton Abbot and Teignmouth when I rounded the curve above Wear Farm and there was the Teign spread out like a picture, calm enough to mirror all of Shaldon and houses on the river Beach in Teignmouth.

The sun was shining directly onto the distant scene, bouncing off the water and melting fields, trees and buildings into gold. I parked my car and just gazed, and as the sun sank further the shadows on this side of the estuary turned everything a gorgeous shade of cool deep green.

As I returned home later in the evening along the same stretch of road, it occurred to me that I'd 'recognised' the image – I'd seen it somewhere before as a picture. I eventually found the picture I'd remembered: it was an image in a book (*Devon – Its Moorlands, Streams and Coasts*, Chatto & Windus, 1930) that F J Widgery had illustrated, and looking at it again I'm certain he was pounced on too.

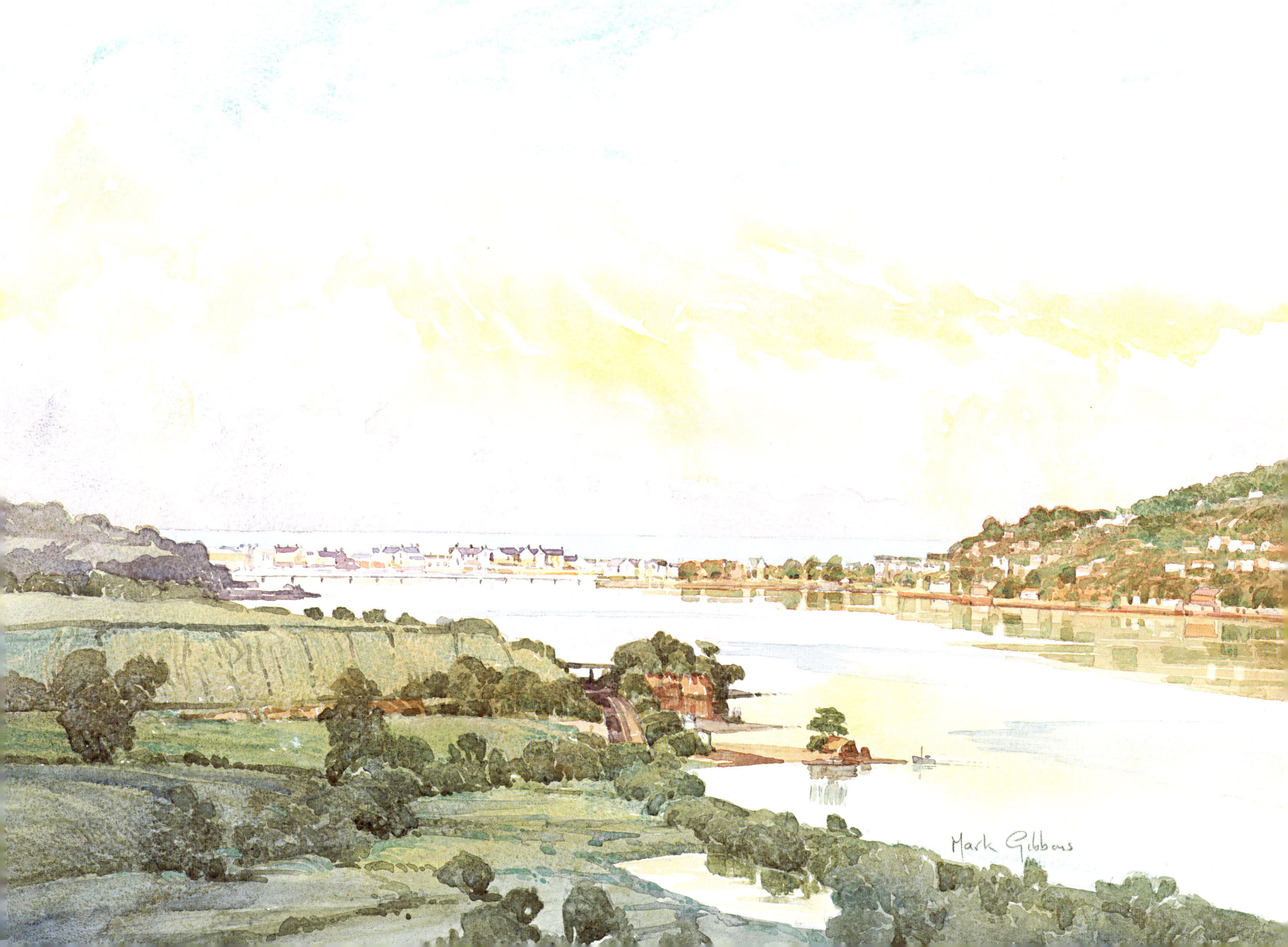
Mark Gibbons

Shaldon Ness at dawn

The Ness is one of the most prominent landmarks along this part of the coast and must have guided many mariners to the safety of the Teign estuary – though as I've found to my cost while canoeing, the currents at the mouth of the Teign can be remarkably fierce when the tide is in full flow.

On the left of the picture you can see the beach huts lined up along the river beach on the Teignmouth side, with the navigation beacon at the end of the point warning of the sand bar at high tide. On the other side of the estuary is the jumble of Shaldon houses that spill down onto the beach. The tree-topped Ness is clearly visible in the background.

I chose to paint the scene at low water because I like the patterns the dark shingle of the Salty makes against the brightly lit water. The painting is composed with a relatively high horizon and a foreground focal point of the twin-keeled sailing boat whose tall mast and reflection divide the picture in a very pleasing way.

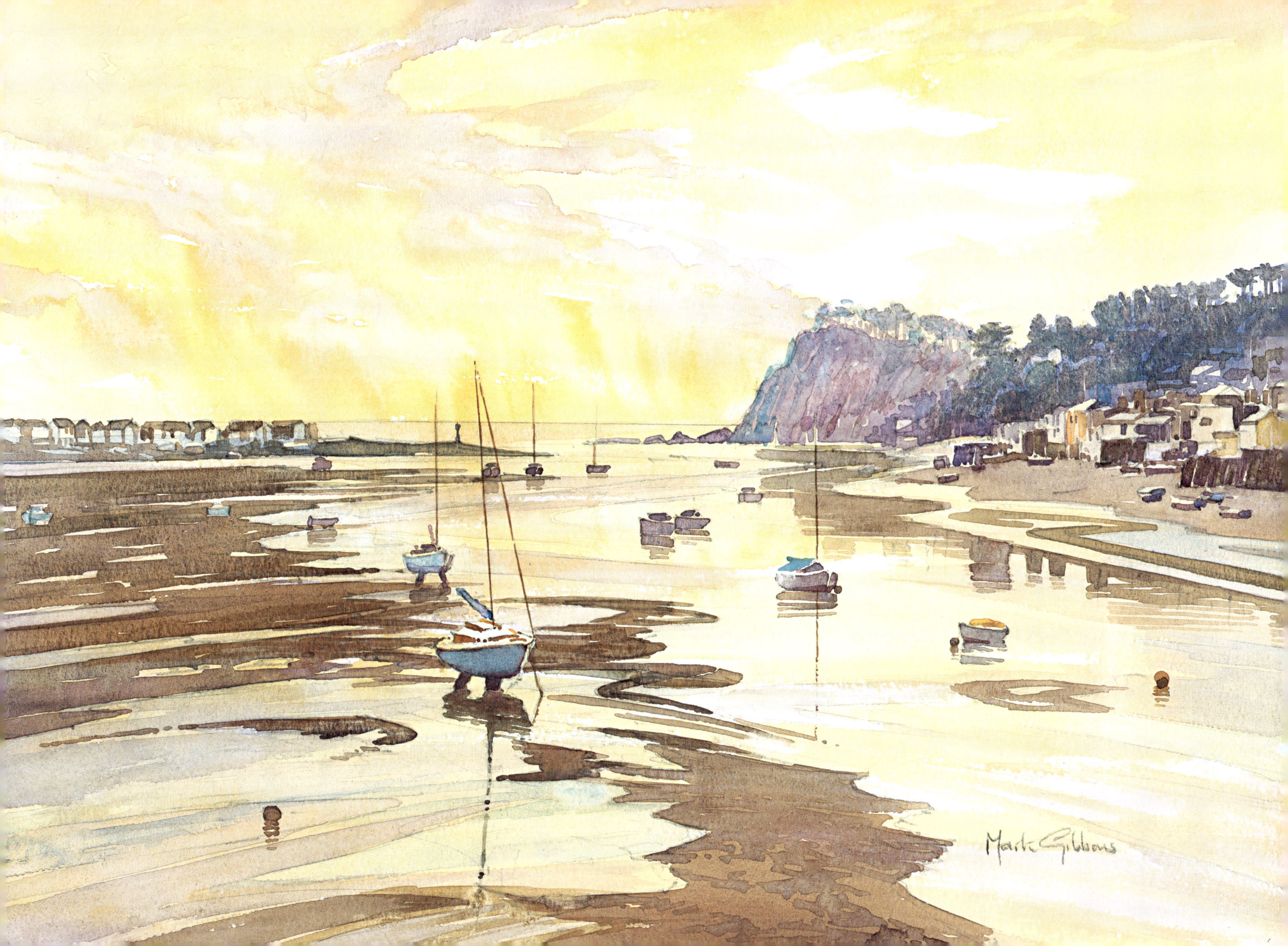
Mark Gibbons

Thatcher Rock, Torquay

Thatcher Rock stands just a few hundred metres off the coast close to Hope's Nose in Torquay. The view in the painting is from Ilsham Marine Drive, just as the road reaches the top of the rise.

Torquay grew from several small hamlets and flourished very quickly indeed even before a train service was established. Eventually the hamlets merged and what undeveloped land there was tended to be confined to the more inaccessible sections of the coast. Thankfully, the picturesque area between Anstey's Cove and Meadfoot Beach is now part of the Coastal Preservation Area and it affords us a glimpse of what Torquay must have looked like before so much of it was buried under hotels.

It is worth mentioning that on the very site where the fir trees grow, there once stood a house called 'Hill Way Close'. In a spirit of great generosity, the owner bequeathed his home to Torbay Council which subsequently pulled it down to allow an unspoiled prospect of the island. The land around the site is now public parkland and offers one of the fairest outlooks in Torbay.

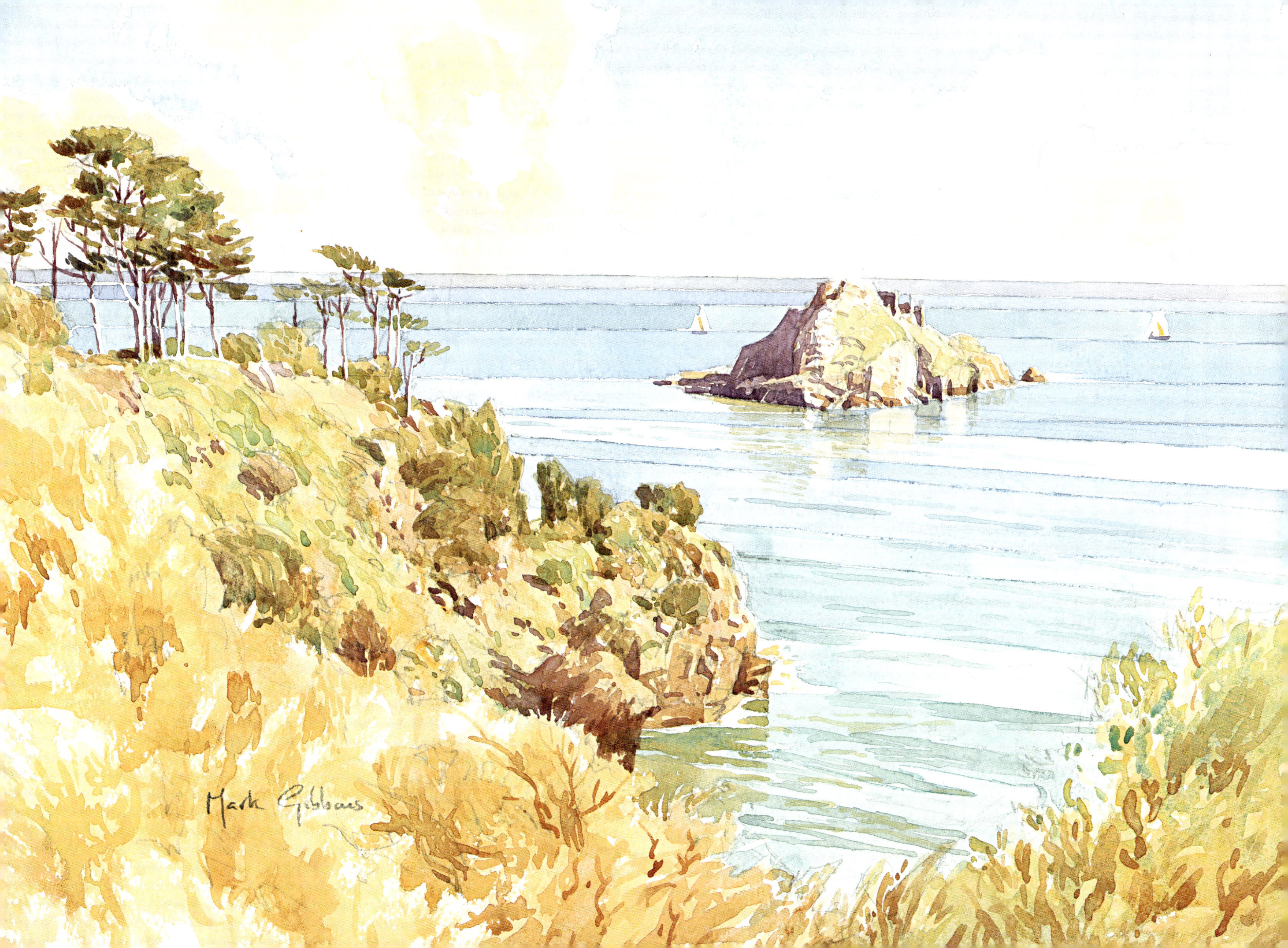
Mark Gibbons

Sailing into Dartmouth

If you gaze out towards the sea from Bayard's Cove, you'll spot one of the most easily recognisable views in Devon. There, silhouetted at the very entrance to Dartmouth, is the famous Dartmouth Castle and, close behind it, the tower of St Petroc's Church.

How many thousands of sailors must have been thankful to pass the Castle on their port bow on their way to the safety of the harbour. It was built in 1481, one of the first in the country to be designed for the use of heavy artillery.

On the other side of the river, the Kingswear side, a smaller castle was built and in times of war, when Dartmouth was threatened, a great barrier chain was drawn across the river mouth, effectively sealing the town off from danger. Any ships that were driven onto the chain by an onshore wind became sitting targets for the great guns set close to water level only a few hundred metres away.

Although the castle can be reached easily by road, I would suggest that on a fine day it is worth taking the small open boat that ferries passengers to and from steps below the sturdy walls. It departs regularly from the town quay. If you're lucky and the wind is just right, you'll arrive there with the taste of salt spray on your lips.

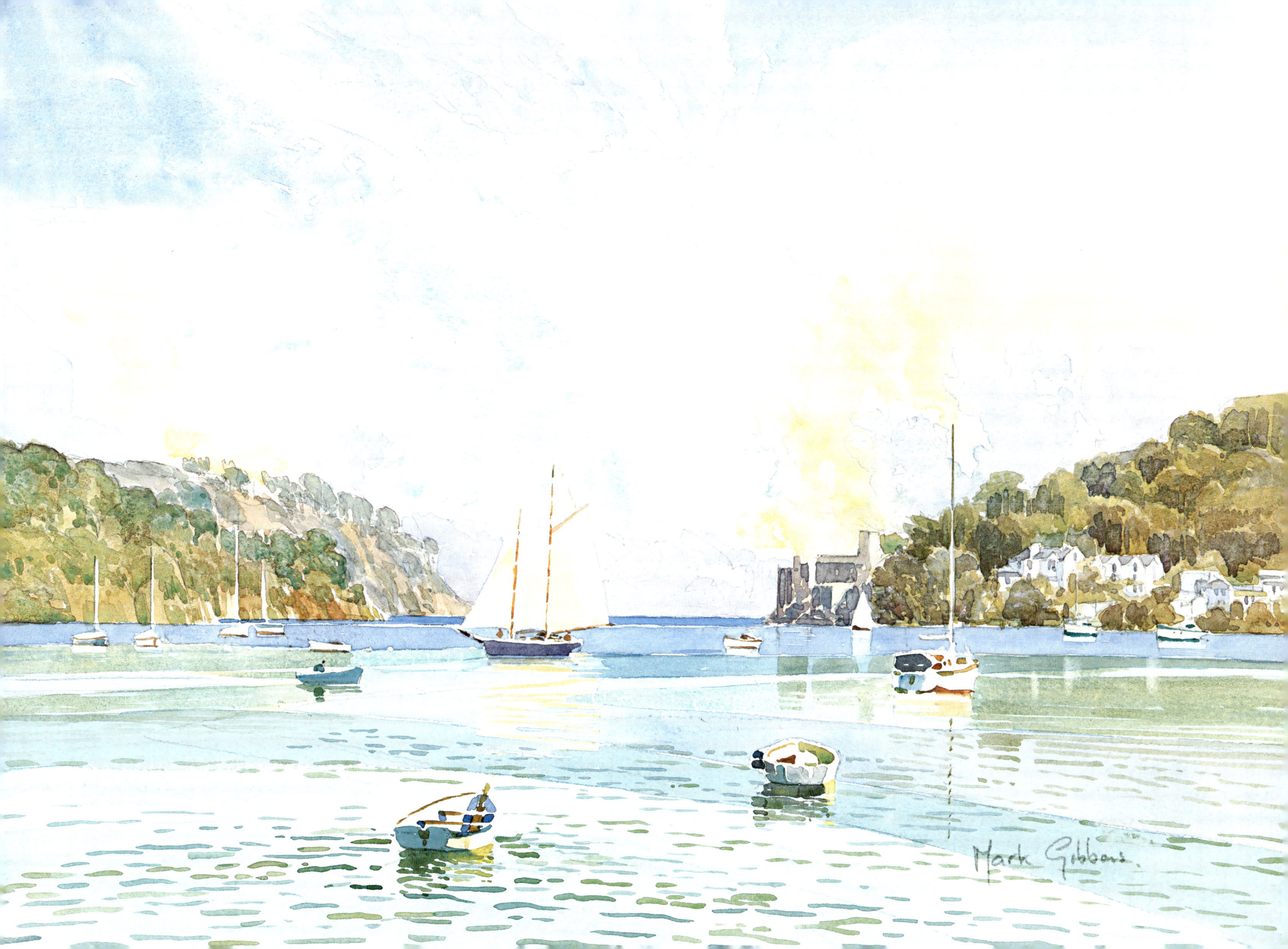
Mark Gibbons

Totnes on the River Dart

Looking up river from Sharpham Drive, you can see the Dart running almost straight north-west to the ancient town of Totnes. Far in the distance the hills rise up to the craggy skyline of Dartmoor.

By the early 1500s, Totnes was even more prosperous than Dartmouth. Road transport was very slow and difficult, and it was easier for merchants to convey their goods down the river than taking them overland to the sea port. Much of the trade was in Devon's famous woollen cloth, and the wealth it generated enabled the great red sandstone tower of St Mary's Church to be built. Standing about 36 metres high, it reaches well above the roofs of the houses.

At the top of the main street (and clearly visible in the painting) is Totnes Castle. The circular stone walls were built in 1326, though the central 'motte' or mound was constructed during Norman times.

There is a well-known print of Totnes by William Turner which is close in viewpoint to mine. To understand the meaning of 'artistic licence', have a look at his picture! You can find a reproduction in *Historic Dart* by Eric Hemery (David & Charles, 1982). The castle is massive and occupies a separate hill of its own, and the church of St Mary looks more than 60 metres high... Never mind, it is still a handsome picture and Turner is, after all, one of England's finest painters.

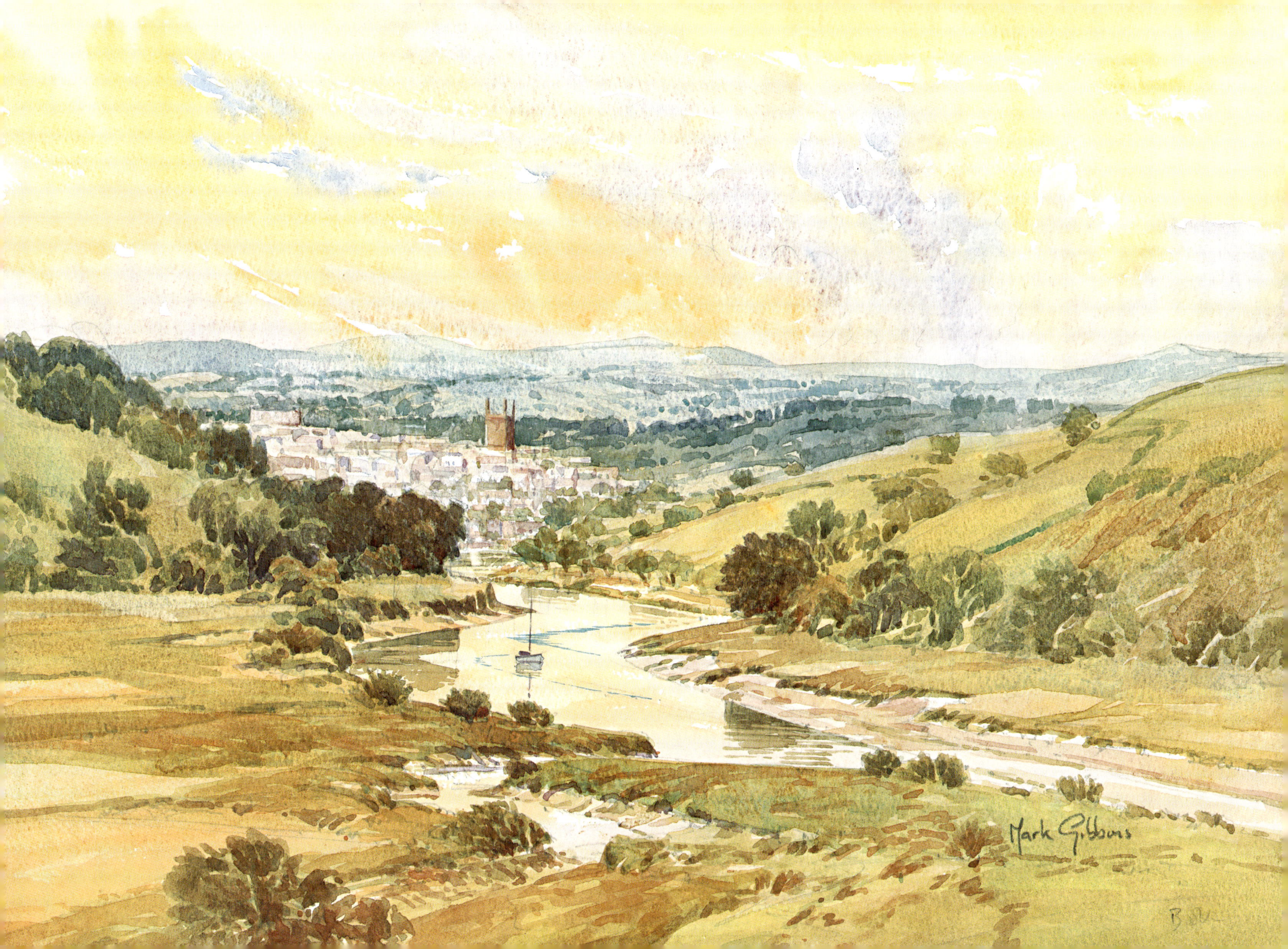
Mark Gibbons

The Maltsters Quay on Bow Creek

Situated opposite Stoke Gabriel, Bow Creek is a tiny tributary of the Dart. At Bow Bridge the Harbourne river flows into it and a quay is sited close to the village of Tuckenhay.

From the late 1700s boats carrying lime and corn used this quay, and they would also have been loaded with cider and malt which were made on the spot and with paper from the mill at Tuckenhay.

When I first visited the place in the mid-1970s it was very run down and neglected, though I was delighted to find cider still being produced there. In 1989 the TV chef Keith Floyd bought the Maltsters Arms just above the quay and he redeveloped it extensively. The Old Winery next door was converted to holiday accommodation and, in keeping with his particular brand of quirky humour, he put life-size models of crocodiles in the creek! The brief colourful years of 'Floyd's Inn (sometimes)' came to an end in 1996.

I'm pleased that the Maltsters Arms has now reclaimed its name and that the new owners have done so much to encourage boats to return to the quay side. The beer and food are excellent and the new pontoon allows easy access by water for a couple of hours either side of high water.

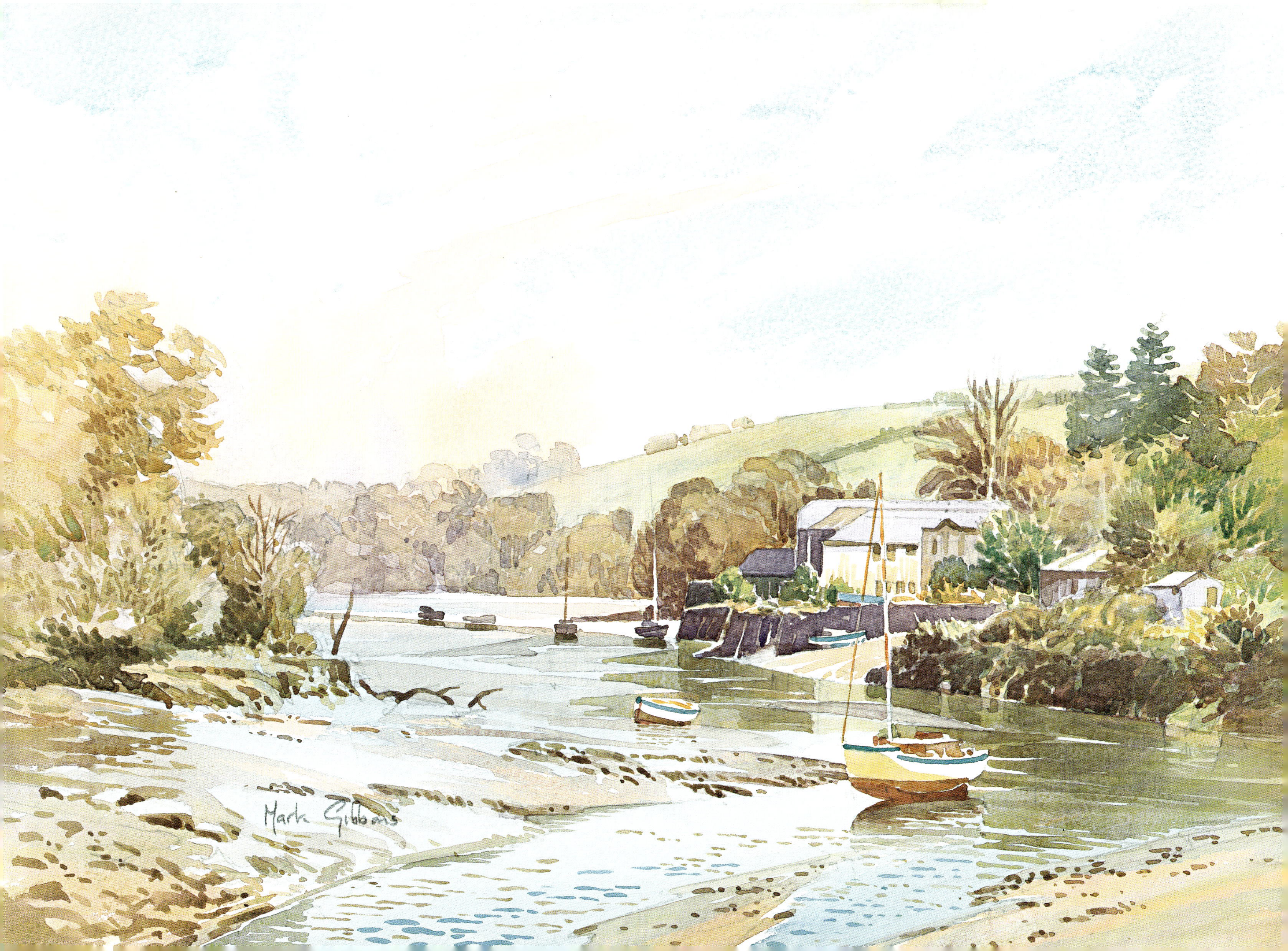
Mark Gibbons

Slapton Ley

Slapton Ley is Devon's largest natural freshwater lake. It is separated from the sea by a four kilometre ridge of shingle which apparently was formed by glacial meltwaters after the last ice age.

The lake is known to have existed for at least a thousand years. Today it is visited by many rare migratory birds (and dozens of birdwatchers!) and has now become a nature reserve. Designated a Site of Special Scientific Interest, it is managed by Slapton Ley Field Centre in Slapton village.

The painting shows the ley calm and serene under an evening sky. In the distance you can just about distinguish the houses of Torcross at the far end of the shingle ridge. On one evening in 1979 it would have looked dramatically different. A ferocious north-easterly gale drove mountainous seas onto the narrow beach. As the tide and wind rose, the waves broke over the ridge, threatening to inundate the lake. The seaward-facing houses in Torcross took a terrible pounding.

I remember going down there the day after the storm. The houses had narrowly escaped being washed away and stood teetering over what had once been a beach, their foundations exposed to the elements and their thatched roofs almost stripped bare. The following year, at great expense, a defensive sea-wall was erected, but given the fate of Hallsands a little further down the coast I wonder how long it will hold.

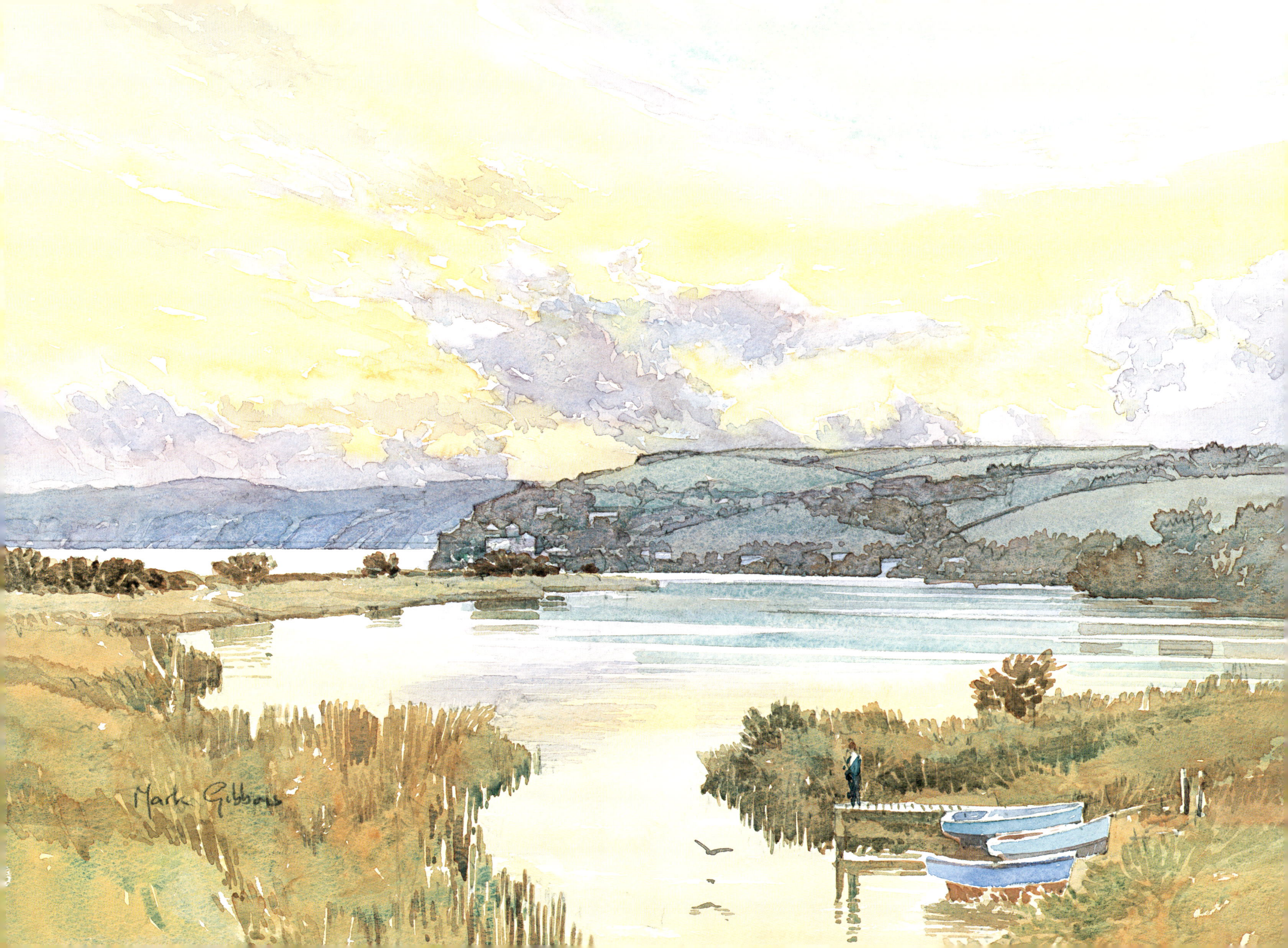
Mark Gibbons

Sailing at Salcombe

Salcombe was once a great shipbuilding town: no fewer than 288 sailing vessels were built here between 1796 and 1912, and hundreds of people were employed making sails and spars.

The smells of pitch, tar and wood shavings have been replaced by the modern aromas of curing fibreglass and Salcombe's own delicious icecream. But there can be no doubt it is still Devon's most thriving sailing centre. Some would even say there are too many boats in Salcombe.

In my painting I've tried to capture some of the zest of dinghy sailing, with boats tacking back and forth across the breezy blue of the estuary off Mill Bay. On the far right is Fort Charles, which saw much service during the Civil War. Behind that in the distance is South Sands.

If you enjoy walking, rather than sailing, there is a wonderful walk that winds up from behind South Sands Hotel and leads to Bolt Head, skirting Starehole Bay. The path follows the edge of the immense craggy cliffs (seen in the background of the picture) and the scenery is breathtaking.

All this area is owned by The National Trust, and the path is well maintained and signposted. In one or two places the climb is quite steep, but I assure you the views are well worth the effort.

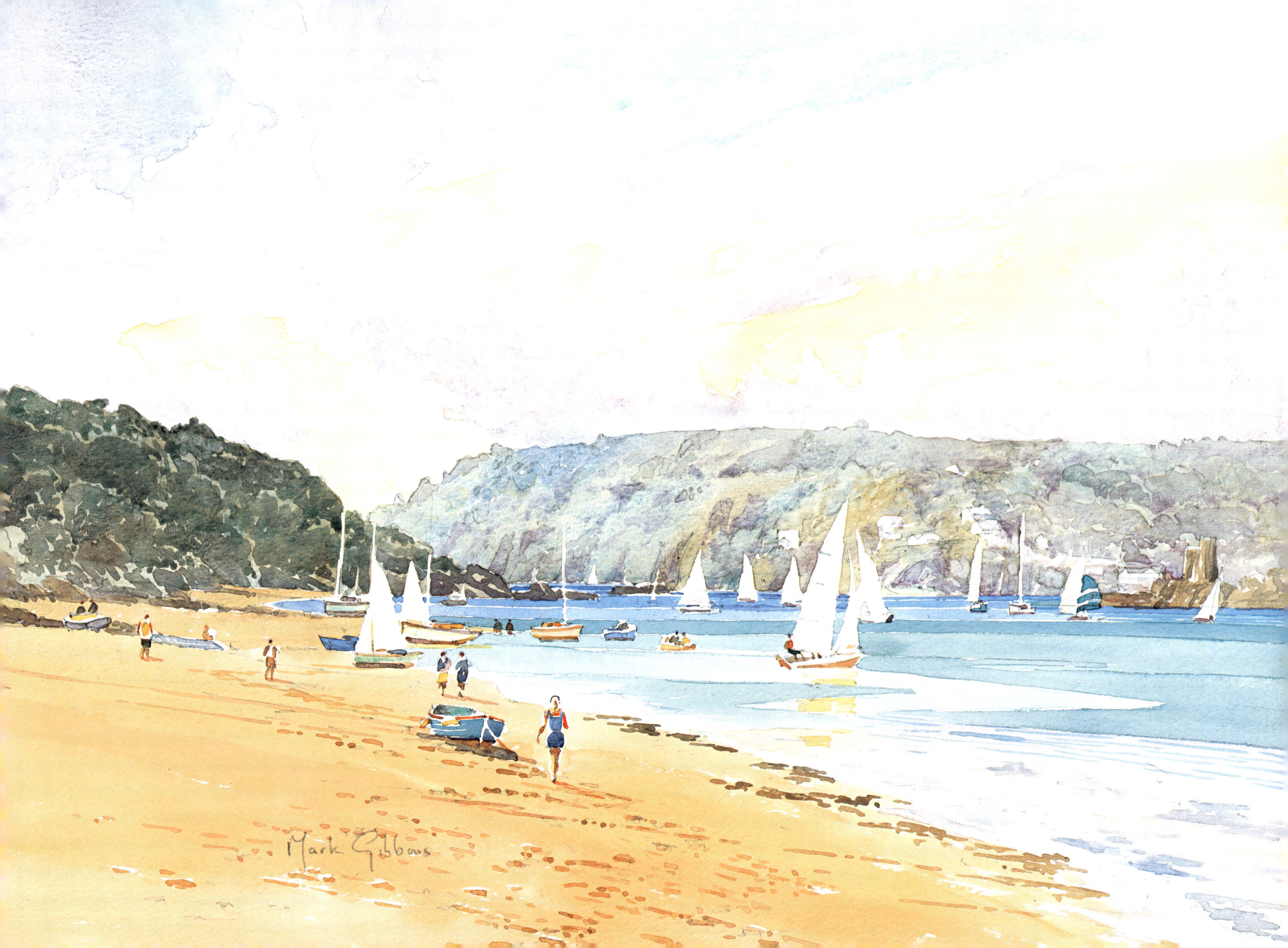
Mark Gibbons

Bowcombe Creek near Kingsbridge

Bowcombe Creek at the northern end of the Kingsbridge estuary is a tiny, hidden away backwater – the sort of place I'm happy to explore while paddling quietly in my Canadian canoe.

I've painted the view looking south on a perfectly still evening. In the distance you can just make out the arches in the road bridge that carries traffic between West Charleton and Kingsbridge. In 1845 a swing bridge was constructed to allow boats to navigate to the head of the creek where slate from Buckland-Tout-Saints was loaded on board. It pivoted by means of a 'race' of twelve cannon balls which act like ball-bearings.

I designed the painting using a limited palette. The green greys of the trees are little more than simple silhouettes with a touch of lighter tone to 'model' them into three-dimensional forms. The colours of the sky and water were also chosen with care. The warmth in the sky above the faraway clouds has been accentuated by a cool green higher up. As for the water, its reflective qualities largely give it its 'wet' look, so I've painted the reflections with small gaps here and there to suggest the slightest of movements on the surface. The gulls skimming down play their part too: they were placed in a particular way to help form a subtle oval shape around which the rest of the picture is built.

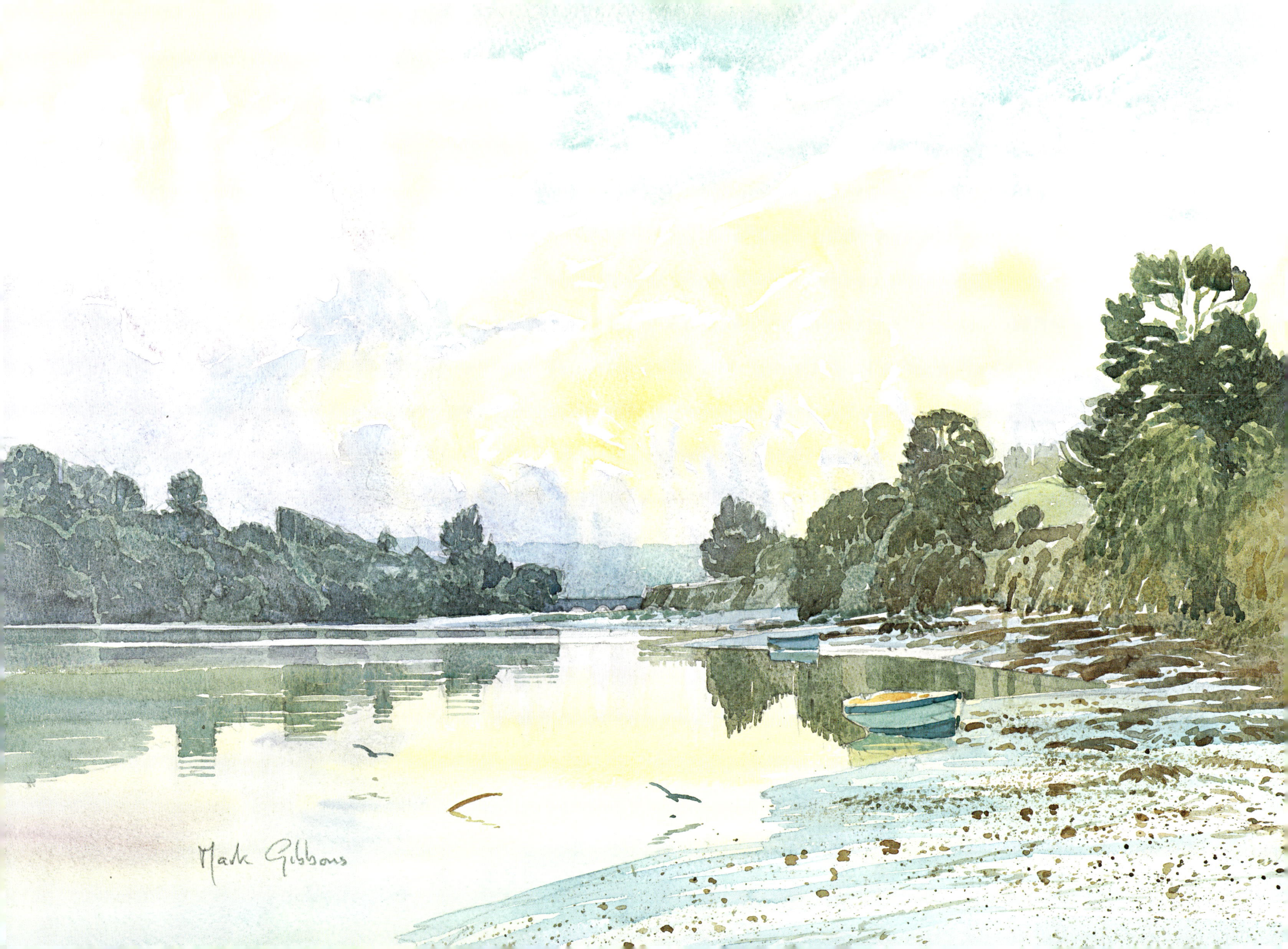
Mark Gibbons

Evening, Kingsbridge Estuary

Should you wish to find this lovely open view of Kingsbridge estuary (though I cannot promise you the perfect summer evening), take the South Pool road from Frogmore and after about 800 metres halt on the brow of the hill. Frogmore creek winds eastwards (to the right of the picture), and beyond Ham Point and Wareham Point an area of the estuary known as Widegates can be seen in the middle distance.

The painting shows the South Hams at its best, with gently rolling farmland of rich red Devon earth and the creeks which give so many small villages their daily tidal connection to the sea. I wanted to convey a feeling of expansiveness, of the great distance that has to be travelled by the eye. The foreground has been kept warm in colour with a path designed to lead off towards the middle distance, and towards the horizon the paint becomes bluer and paler, mimicking the effect of atmospheric perspective.

It's a good picture (I think!), but not quite as good as being there!

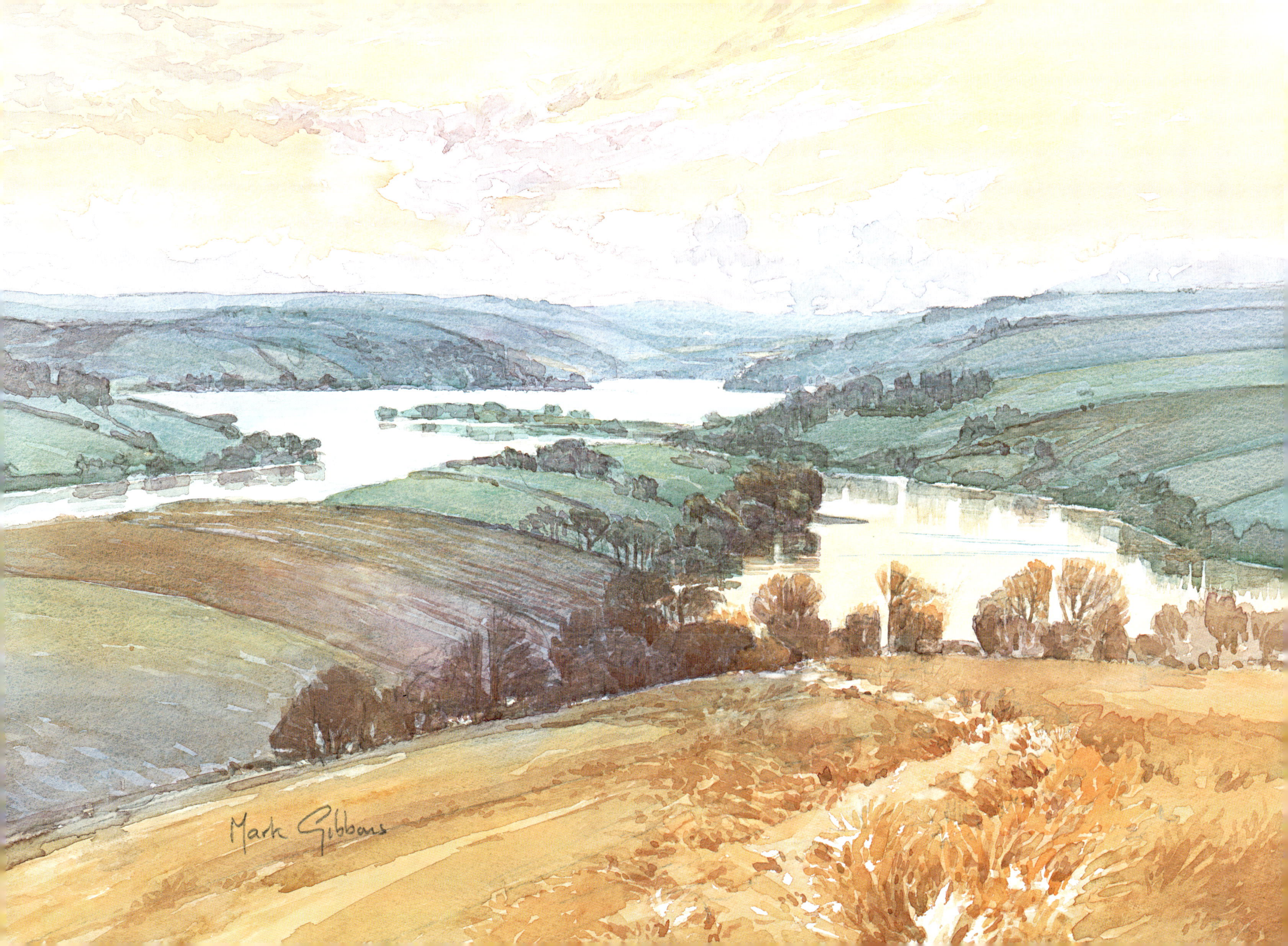
Mark Gibbons

Thurlestone Rock

Thurlestone Rock – 'the rock with the hole in it' – can be seen from a great distance along this part of coastline. Some local history books suggest it was called Thurleston long before the village ever came into being, and that in effect it gave its name to the settlement.

Looking at the painting it's just about possible to identify Burgh Island, with its famous hotel, and to the right is Warren Point with the sunlit green of Thurleston's outstanding golf course.

However, the subject of the painting is really none of these things. It is more the shifting quality of the light. The clouds are moving briskly inland, the sunlight momentarily illuminating the surf and throwing deep shadows under the Rock. The sea in the foreground is shallow over sand and the seaweed shows purple and blurred under the water. In the distance the sunlit sea is almost a yellow rather than a blue. All is movement and change.

If these ideas come across in the picture, then I'm happy; if not, well you can always say 'It's a painting of Thurleston Rock'!

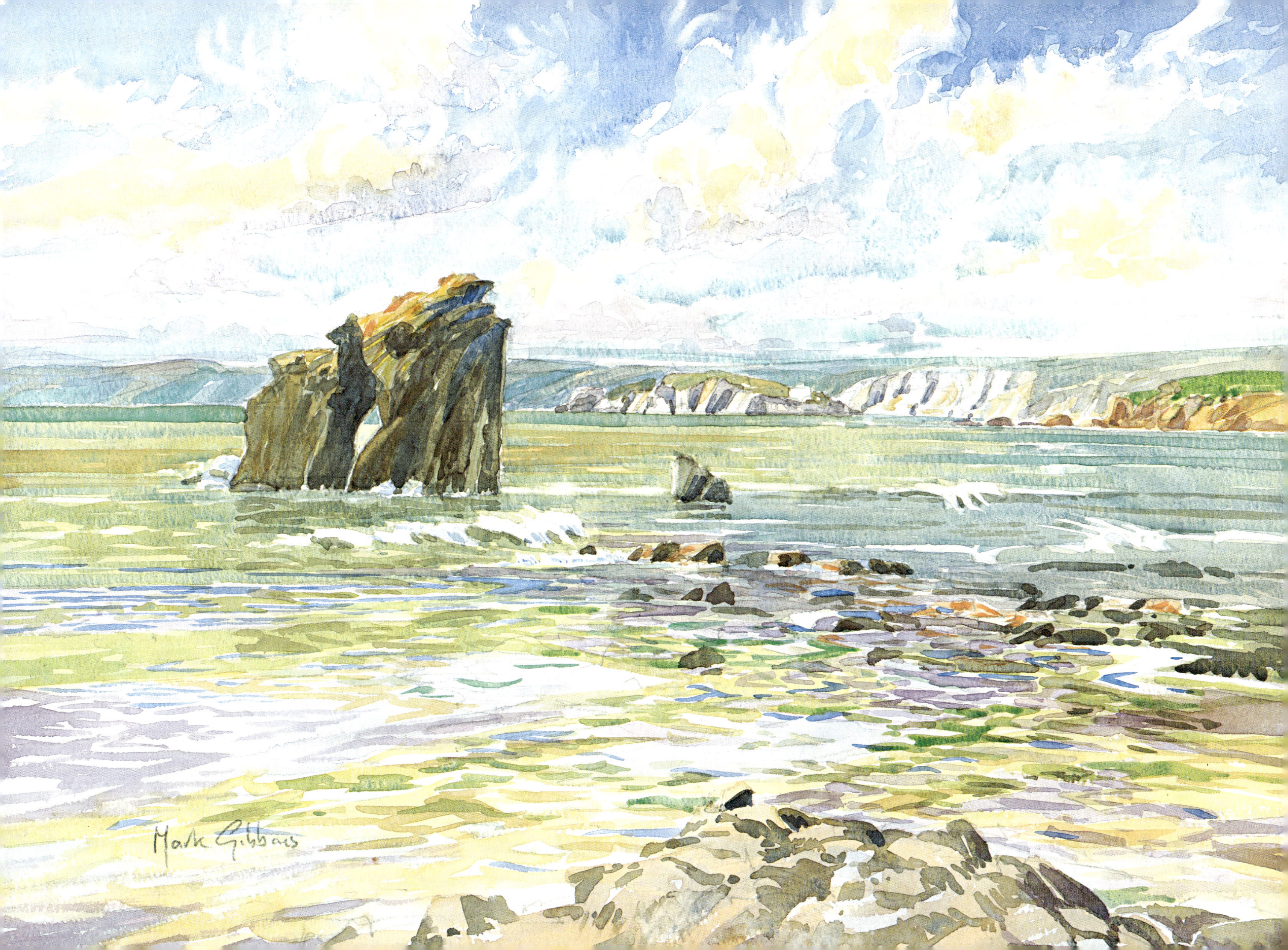
Mark Gibbons

Burgh Island

This particular view of the island can be found by walking from Thurleston and following the coast path up along the golf course to where the headland overlooks Bigbury Bay.

At low tide the island is linked to the mainland by a narrow stretch of firm sand and it is possible to stroll out to it. At high tide the journey becomes something of an adventure, for there is a 'sea tractor' (especially built for the job) which drives through the waves, ferrying passengers to and fro.

On the island's summit are the remains of a huer's hut that was last used during the time of the pilchard industry. The 'huer' kept a lookout for the shoals of fish as they came into the bay. The Pilchard Inn, dated 1336, is the only other link with this part of the island's history.

In 1929 Archibold Nettlefold built the large white art deco hotel, planning to make the place into an English Monte Carlo. During its heyday it attracted many glamorous visitors, Noël Coward and Agatha Christie among them. The books *And then there were none* and *Evil under the sun* are said to have been inspired by the location.

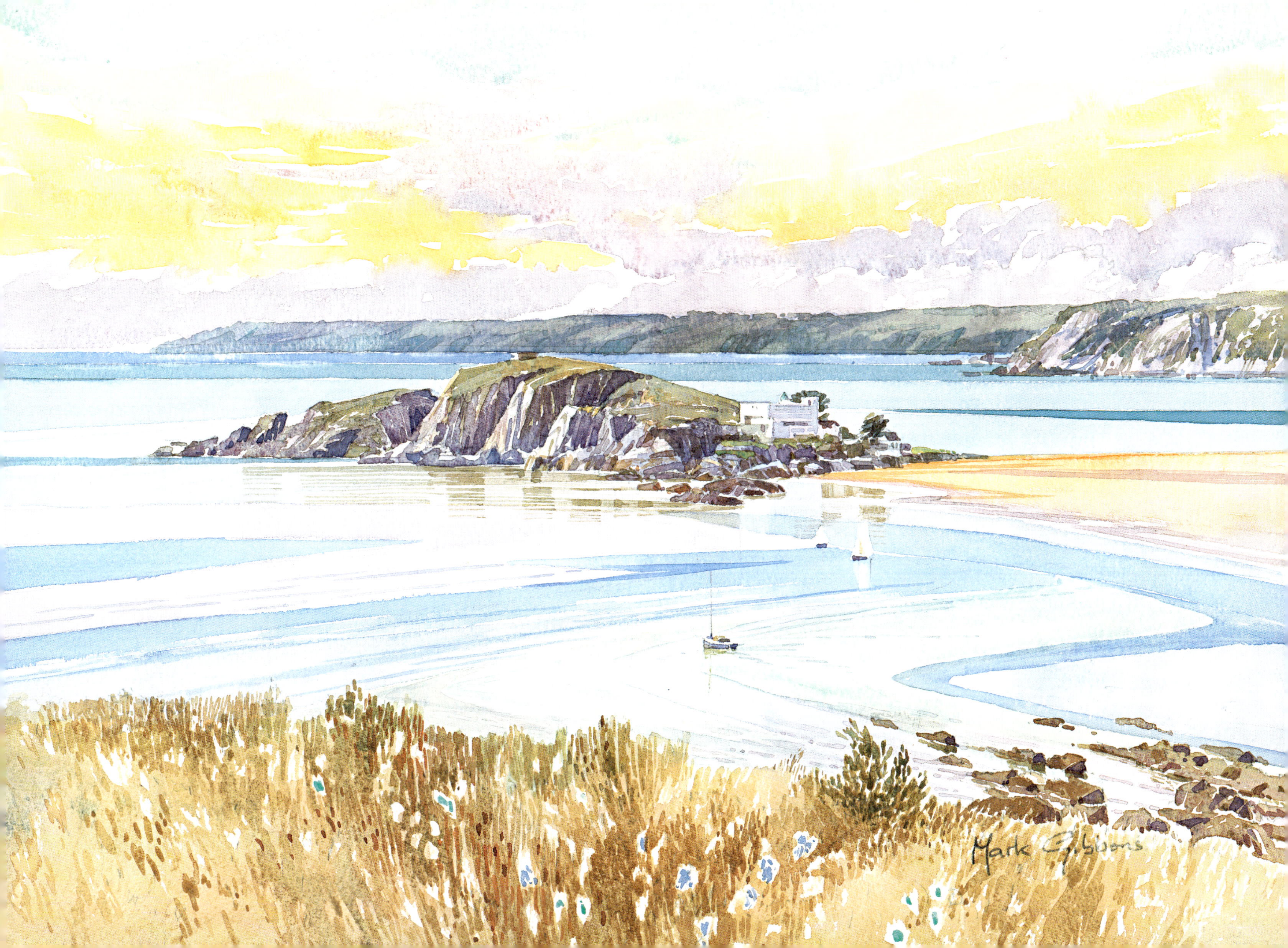
Mark Gibbons

Jenkins' Quay at Bantham

The boat house on the Ham at Bantham must surely be one of the most photographed thatched buildings in South Devon. It looks so ancient and so much a part of the landscape that you'd be forgiven for thinking it is at least several hundred years old. It was in fact built for Henry Jenkins in 1912, though the quay it stands on is much older.

The boat house was erected on the site of the old ferry keeper's cottage – it is known that a certain Sally Andrews ran a small ferry across to Cockleridge on the far side and that she died at the age of 85 in the year 1885. There is still a ferry that runs during the summer months, though it operates from Coronation Quay a little further up the estuary.

While the old building looks snug and well protected, the power of the seas that lie behind it should not be underestimated. In recent years it has been known for waves to break right over the top of the Ham, and on one occasion the sea ran in through the back of the boat house and out through the front!

Having painted around this area for several decades, I've noticed that the large stand of fir trees which grew at the back of the quay has now totally disappeared. Let's hope the boat house, much admired by both locals and visitors, does not share the same fate.

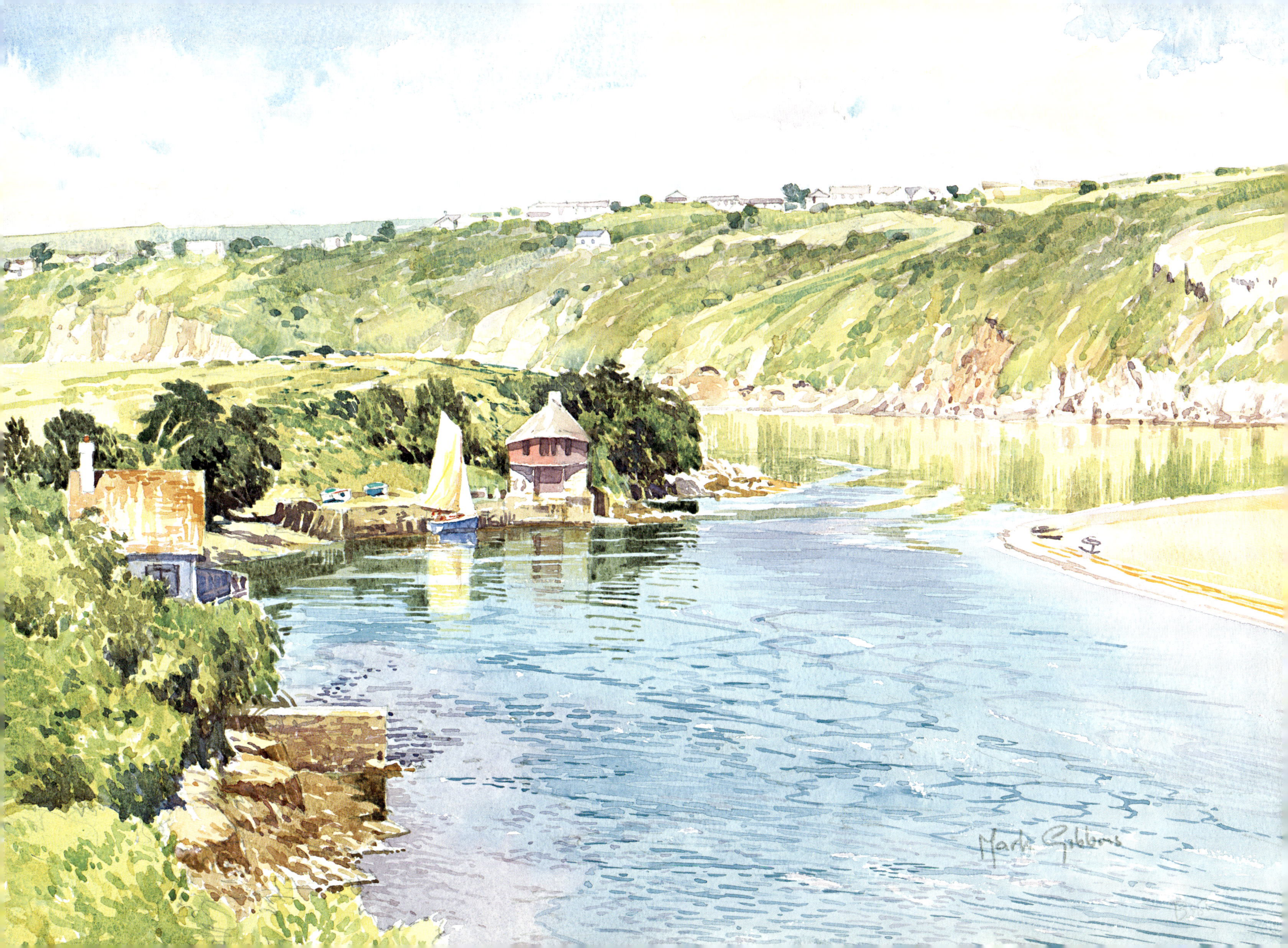
Mark Gibbons

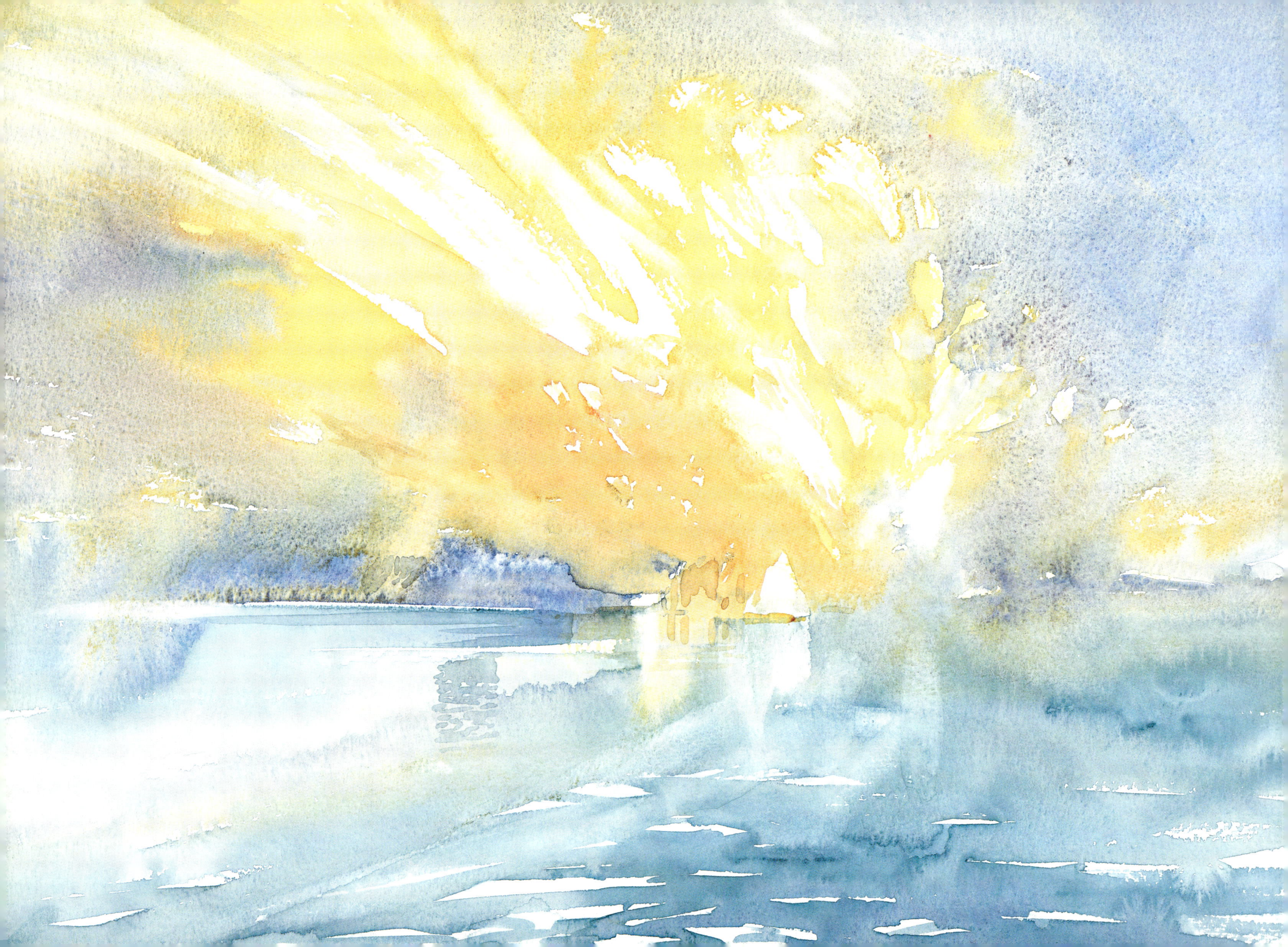